SECRET WORLD
— OF THE —
NINJA

WRITTEN BY
BETH LANDIS HESTER

CONTENTS

INTRODUCTION

BALANCE IS EVERYTHING.

Where there is light, there is darkness.
Where there is goodness, evil looms. And whenever
evil strikes, there will always be Ninja to counter it.
Using the ancient art of Spinjitzu and their elemental
powers—fire, ice, earth, and lightning—these
protectors of peace never back down.

But this wasn't always the way: Once upon a time,
the heroes now known as Ninja were ordinary kids.
They ate pizza, played video games, and never
thought about what the future would hold.
But with the guidance of Sensei Wu, they are
learning to harness their true potential—fighting
for good, protecting all of Ninjago… and still
making it home in time for pizza.

Are you ready to unlock the
secrets of the Ninja?

SENSEI WU

SENSEI WU IS dedicated to passing on his wisdom to a new generation. He believes that inner strength is as important as Spinjitzu skills, so training sessions always end with wise words for the Ninja and a cup of tea for him. Peaceful Wu uses his staff for just one cause: defending Ninjago.

THREE SUGARS, PLEASE!

Sensei Wu is always preparing a restorative cup of tea in his trademark blue teapot. He is rarely without a cup in hand as he watches over his pupils and instructs them in the ways of the Ninja.

Traditional conical hat shades eyes in heat of battle

"THE BEST WAY TO DEFEAT YOUR ENEMY IS TO MAKE HIM YOUR FRIEND."
SENSEI WU

DATA FILE

Known for:
Wisdom

Favorite weapon:
Staff of the Dragons

Likes:
Peace and quiet

Dislikes:
Cold tea

IS IT TEA TIME?

STYLISH SENSEI

Zane describes Wu's dark kimono as "most extraordinary," and he is right! Its golden symbols provide a powerful protection spell that once saved Wu from his evil brother, Garmadon. Wu still wears it today—being good never goes out of fashion.

DID YOU KNOW?

Sensei Wu is the son of the First Spinjitzu Master, the legendary hero who created Ninjago. Wu has vowed to uphold his father's legacy, and protect the land.

CALM TEACHER

Sensei Wu invites four young pupils to join his dojo in a remote monastery. He sees great potential in them, but knows they rely on him to provide structure, lessons, and a guiding hand if they are to unlock their true potential.

WU THE WARRIOR

eaceful, wise, old—these re all words that come o mind when the Ninja hink of Sensei Wu. on't underestimate this xperienced fighter though; Vu's Spinjitzu moves re as sharp as ever!

Shoulder armor provides much needed protection

Golden version of Wu's Nin-jo staff

A NINJA IS...

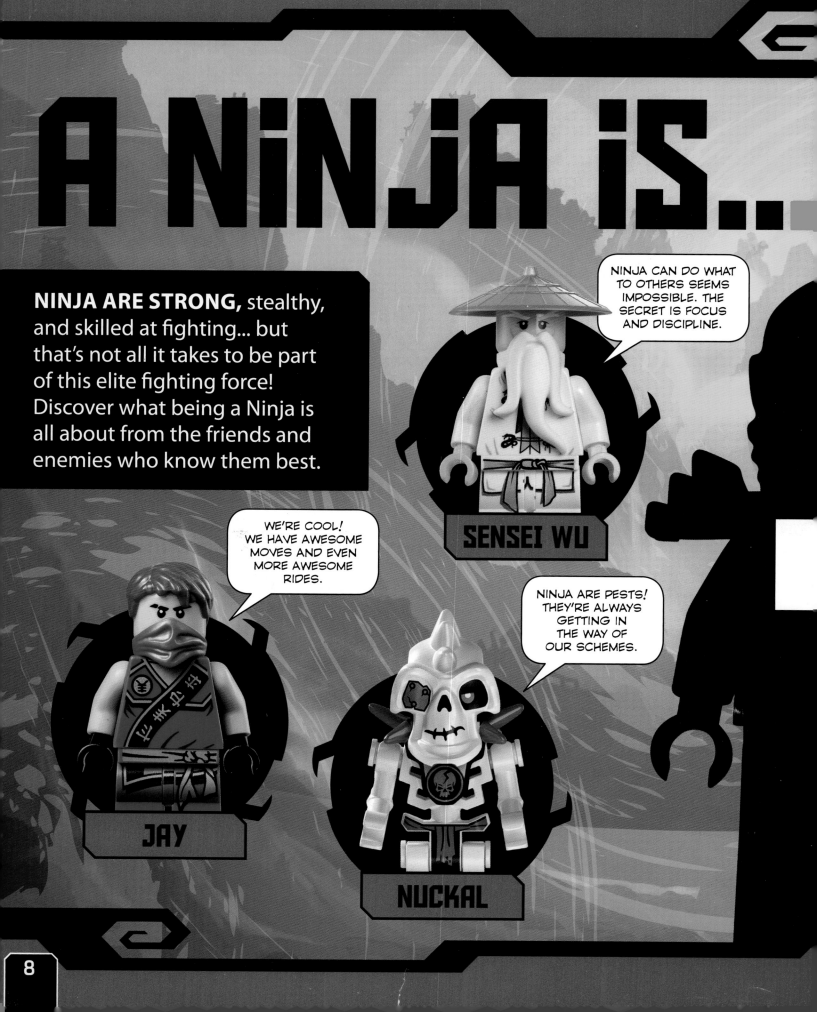

NINJA ARE STRONG, stealthy, and skilled at fighting... but that's not all it takes to be part of this elite fighting force! Discover what being a Ninja is all about from the friends and enemies who know them best.

NINJA CAN DO WHAT TO OTHERS SEEMS IMPOSSIBLE. THE SECRET IS FOCUS AND DISCIPLINE.

SENSEI WU

WE'RE COOL! WE HAVE AWESOME MOVES AND EVEN MORE AWESOME RIDES.

NINJA ARE PESTS! THEY'RE ALWAYS GETTING IN THE WAY OF OUR SCHEMES.

JAY

NUCKAL

KAi

BEFORE BECOMING THE Ninja of Fire, Kai used flames to forge weapons in his family's blacksmith shop. Now, Kai must learn to control his fiery temper and think before he leaps into action. Wu teaches him patience and red-hot Spinjitzu moves.

PROTECTIVE BROTHER

Kai's sister Nya is all the family Kai has got. Nya can stand up for herself, but Kai is determined to keep her safe. He even keeps a watchful eye on his friend Jay, who develops a crush on Nya.

I'M ON FIRE!

"THINK YOU CAN TAKE THE HEAT?"

KAi

Red face mask hides Kai's identity

DATA FILE

- **Known for:**
  Confidence, bravery
- **Favorite weapon:**
  Sword of Fire
- **Likes:**
  Action and excitement
- **Dislikes:**
  Losing at video games

OLD SCHOOL

High-tech gizmos and tricky computer code? No thanks! Kai's years in the blacksmith shop taught him to respect traditional weapons. He prefers blades and swords to buttons and switches any day (well, apart from video games).

MEETING WU

Kai meets Sensei Wu when the wise leader comes looking for a valuable map. It shows the hiding place of four powerful Golden Weapons that belonged to the First Spinjitzu Master. It has been hidden in Kai's blacksmith shop for many years.

Chart counts enemies defeated

Wide shields protect flanks

DID YOU KNOW?

Kai has a mysterious scar across one eye, from long before he became a Ninja. No one, not even his sister Nya, knows how he got it.

Golden blades fire forward

ROAD WARRIOR

Kai says he doesn't like technology, but when his elemental powers conjure this high-tech Blade Cycle, he can't wait to take it for a spin. With golden blades and scorching speed, this menacing machine has all the tools he needs to race after his enemies in a blaze of glory.

SO, YOU WANT TO BE A NINJA?

SENSEI WU KNOWS that a Ninja must be ready for danger at any moment, so there is no time to play in his dojo! There is only time for training (and tea, of course). Do you have what it takes?

DEDICATION

Ninja must always be up and ready to dedicate their day to training. Sensei Wu wakes the Ninja every morning with the not-so-gentle sound of a gong. According to Wu, his father—the First Spinjitzu Master—was always up before sunrise and he never complained!

"WATCH AND LEARN, BROTHERS..."
ZANE

PATiENCE

At the monastery, a rotating robotic obstacle course imitates an enemy attack. Mastering it requires speed, agility... and a few bumps on the head until practice makes perfect!

不屈

正義

忍者 忍者

FOCUS

Concentration is key to perfecting the quick reactions a Ninja needs in battle. Some of the Ninja struggle with achieving the right level of focus, but Zane is Sensei's star pupil. Or, perhaps he has just gone into standby mode.

TEAM SPiRiT

Training as a group allows Kai, Jay, Cole, and Zane to practice fighting side by side —they'll need to know how to support each other when battling their enemies. It also takes more than one Ninja to pull Wu's heavy rickshaw up the mountain, back to the dojo.

THE SKELETON ARMY

GET READY TO RATTLE THOSE BONES!

TOUGH BUT DIMWITTED, these boneheaded Skulkins have escaped the Underworld and are ready to destroy Ninjago. Whoever wears the mystical bone helmet that controls these skeletal soldiers has a powerful force at their command. The Skulkins attack with brute force—but not much brainpower.

I'VE GOT A BONE TO PICK WITH YOU

BONEZAI
Bonezai's vehicles and inventions keep the skeletons on the move toward their next target.

FRAKJAW
Like Kai, Frakjaw is strongly linked with the Fire element—but he doesn't have the Ninja's spark of brilliance.

SAMUKAI
This bony bunch is ruled by four-armed Samukai—the ruthless king of the Underworld. Samukai's extra arms and large head make him even spookier-looking than the skeletons he leads—and that's saying something!

CHOPOV
This menacing mechanic uses his simple tools to repair vehicles and slash enemies down to size.

KRAZI

Look out for this battle-crazed Skulkin! From his toes to the tip of his jester's hat, he's focused on one thing: fighting!

KRUNCHA

Kruncha is one of the more skilled skeletons. He has a knack for driving and a habit for getting into trouble.

WYPLASH

This sneaky skeleton is wiser than most. He also has the creepy ability to turn his head all the way around!

NUCKAL

Nuckal is proof that you don't need brilliance to lead: As a general, his main talent is sheer strength.

Catapult arm fires missiles

Scary skull design

Flaming exhaust

SKULL TRUCK

Driven by Nuckal and Kruncha, this rugged vehicle can roll over just about anything. Its huge wheels crunch over tough terrain and its sturdy frame bursts through obstacles—and watch out for bone-crunching ammo being flung from its top arm!

Resilient tires can withstand great speeds

LORD GARMADON

WHO IS LORD GARMADON? He has been many things: An innocent child poisoned by the Great Devourer's bite, a young husband and father, and a power-hungry warlord. Who knows what this complicated character will become next!

BAD BEGINNINGS

As children, Garmadon and Wu trained happily together under the guidance of their father, the First Spinjitzu Master. The brothers became enemies when Garmadon was bitten by a snake and infected with evil.

> ## "MY DARKEST DREAM WILL BECOME REALITY!"
> ## LORD GARMADON

One of four hands for wielding multiple weapons

DATA FILE

- ✳ **Known for:**
  Playing dirty
- ✖ **Favorite weapon:**
  Garmadon dreams of combining the Golden Weapons into one Megaweapon
- 👍 **Likes:**
  Power and glory
- 👎 **Dislikes:**
  The Great Devourer

DID YOU KNOW?

Lord Garmadon is a little odd. He eats Condensed Evil (black slime full of maggots) and sunbathes in thunderstorms!

LEND ME A HAND?

EVIL EVOLUTION

The evil inside Garmadon shows on the outside: venom from the snake that bit him turns his eyes red and gives him terrifying fangs. He once had two arms, but he later grows extra arms as part of his quest to master the four Golden Weapons.

Nin-jo (bamboo stick)

SIBLING RIVALRY

Battles between Sensei Wu and Lord Garmadon are fierce. Blow by blow, spin by spin, these two Spinjitzu masters can match every move the other makes. Who will win in this epic struggle between light and dark, good and evil?

DEVIOUS SCHEMES

Clever Garmadon anticipates the feelings and actions of others—a gift that he uses to trick and sneak his way to power. When he kidnaps Nya, he knows that Kai will come to her rescue, putting the Golden Sword of Fire at risk—exactly what Garmadon wants.

Thunder Bolt weapon

BATTLE AT THE DARK FORTRESS!

A BATTLE RAGES for control of four powerful Golden Weapons at Garmadon's Underworld lair. Odds are against the Ninja: Enemy gunners are overhead, giant spiders hang nearby, and Samukai has three of his four hands armed and ready to attack. Can the Ninja and Sensei Wu prevail?

A giant skull spider looms over the battle

NO ONE MESSES WITH MY SISTER!

GREEDY GARMADON

Garmadon desperately wants to possess the legendary Golden Weapons—but he knows he's not yet strong enough to hold all four at once. Instead, he tricks others into gathering the weapons, fighting off his enemies, and helping him escape the Underworld.

Bones are everywhere in this Underworld fortress

NINJA TO THE RESCUE

The Ninja use their elemental powers to create Spinjitzu tornadoes that flatten their enemies. These swirling forces combine to make an even more powerful weapon: The Tornado of Creation sucks in everything nearby and uses them to create something new.

Skull missiles are launched from the tower gunnery

NYA ESCAPES

Nya was kidnapped to lure the Ninja into this terrible battle—but she's far from helpless. The moment she's free, Nya joins the fight against the Skulkin.

SAMUKAI VS. WU

With two sets of arms, Samukai wields three of the four Golden Weapons— and he's determined to complete the set. Wu must defeat him before he finds the fourth, the Sword of Fire, and masters their power.

WHAT DO NINJA WEAR?

NINJA GEAR IS designed to allow the Ninja to perform their most energetic Spinjitzu moves. They have different uniforms for every occasion, but Kai just thinks everything looks extra-awesome in red!

DAPPER GENTS

When the Ninja go undercover in a dance competition, their instructor—Cole's dad—gives them these snazzy suits. The Ninja aren't impressed.

STARTING OUT

Sensei Wu provides the Ninja with this outfit and a rope belt at the start of their training. Zane's snow-white robes and golden Ice emblem reflect his frosty powers.

FLYING OUTFIT

The Ninja have gi that show each of their dragons breathing his elemental power. Jay's bright blue robes show his dragon, Wisp, breathing lightning.

TRAINING GEAR

An armored mask and shielded front offer protection when the Ninja train. It's too bulky for real battles, but Kai welcomes any barrier from the blows of the training machines.

BATTLE READY

Perfect for fighting, this lightly armored gi has protection in just the right places—on the shoulders and forehead. The silver metal looks great with Cole's black robes.

TRUE POTENTIAL

When the Ninja reach their true potential their elemental powers flow through their bodies and enhance their abilities. Zane is the first Ninja to unlock this talent.

TEMPLE OF LIGHT

These very ornate, mainly black suits are a symbol of the new, even greater elemental powers the Ninja receive in the Temple of Light. Looking flashy, Jay!

ON THE RUN

Cyrus Borg supplies these suits on the eve of a new battle—to disguise the Ninja and to help them to fight the Overlord. Kai likes that he no longer has to mess up his hair.

DID YOU KNOW?

A Ninja's robes are often referred to as gi. They are recognized across Ninjago as the traditional clothing of these brave warriors.

SCHOOL UNIFORM

The Ninja take jobs as teachers when Wu opens his academy. They swap their masks and gi for sweaters and blazers for a school trip.

DRESSED TO WIN

When the Ninja enter the Tournament of Elements, they pack two outfits. The lightweight, sleeveless robes allow for quick moves in the competition, while their heavy-duty robes are crammed with tools the Ninja may need.

JAY

JAY IS FUN LOVING, fast-talking, and full of energy. He knows a witty one-liner is the perfect way to follow a Spinjitzu strike. That's not the only way Jay adds electricity: His lightning-fast reflexes and technical expertise are a serious asset to his team.

FAMILY RESEMBLANCE

Jay's parents, Ed and Edna Walker, turn other people's trash into cool inventions—including their customized clunker of a car, which they love taking out on adventures.

> "MIGHT AS WELL GO DOWN LAUGHING!"
> JAY

Yellow Techno Blade resembles a chainsaw

Robes have lightning strike decoration

DATA FILE

- ✹ **Known for:**
  Corny jokes
- ✕ **Favorite weapon:**
  Nunchucks of Lightning
- 👍 **Likes:**
  Hanging out with Nya
- 👎 **Dislikes:**
  Bad hair days

> WHAT COULD GO WRONG?

AMAZING INVENTOR
Where others see sticks and paper, Jay sees a way to fly! Like his parents, handy Jay can turn odds and ends into amazing inventions. His creations have helped the Ninja out of countless scrapes, and a great imagination gives Jay the power to solve any problem.

TORM FIGHTER
the cockpit of his super-fast plane, inja of Lightning Jay is a force of ature. The Storm Fighter has the ower to attack as well as defenses protect—if an enemy is on Jay's il, he can streak away through the ouds like a lightning bolt!

Flight deck

DID YOU KNOW?
Jay was the first of the four Ninja to be found by Sensei Wu, and was the first to master Spinjitzu.

Slim fuselage for speed

SWEETHEARTS
On their first date, Jay tries to dazzle Nya with fancy clothes, a well-oiled hairdo, and partially true stories of his own incredible feats. But the pair really connect when Nya tells him the best true story of all: She likes him just the way he is!

WHERE DO NINJA LIVE?

THE NINJA HAVE called lots of places home, but the perfect dojo is very hard to find. Ninja need a home that's large enough to train in, well-equipped, and—most importantly for Jay—has somewhere to play video games!

The Ninja's original headquarters had great training equipment, but not much space. Cole insisted on creating a strict rota system for the only bathroom after Zane burst in when he was least expecting it!

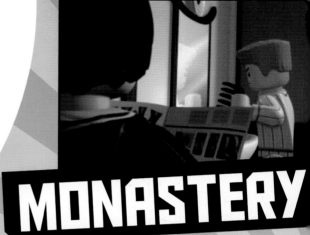

MONASTERY

DESTINY'S BOUNTY

It took some hard work to transform this old ship into a high-tech flying dojo. After some sprucing up and computer upgrades, it was a sight to behold... until it was damaged in battle.

MOBILE BASE

It pays to have a workshop, garage, and control center close at hand when preparing for a battle. When the Ninja venture to Master Chen's island, Nya follows in a vehicle that houses all the weapons and vehicles they may need.

高速

Nya designed the mobile base herself, including its handy robot driver. She has made sure it is well armored and easy to pack up—perfect for making a quick getaway when enemies get too close!

THE SERPENTINE

AFTER CENTURIES OF warring amongst themselves, the five Serpentine tribes were entombed underground by the angry residents of Ninjago. Now, a young boy called Lloyd has set them free—and with terrifying powers like these, no one in Ninjago can sleep easily!

YOU'RE HISSSTORY!

ANACONDRAI

According to legend, this ancient race of snakes is the most powerful and deadly of all. The only surviving member of the species is cunning Pythor. He has the ability to make himself invisible, which he uses to sneak away after convincing others to do his bidding.

YOU SAY MEAN LIKE IT IS A BAD THING...

VENOMARI

A spray of toxic venom from these green meanies causes weird visions. Victims might think they see a safe path where there isn't one—a dangerous mistake in the deadly toxic bog where the Venomari live.

LOOK INTO MY EYESSS...

HYPNOBRAI

Don't look too closely at these mesmerizing rattlers! One glance into their glowing eyes, and enemies are hypnotized. Then they are forced to do whatever the ssslithering sssnakes sssay. Their general, Skales, is an expert in the snake martial art, Fang-Kwon-Do.

MAYBE WE'VE BITTEN OFF MORE THAN WE CAN CHEW?

SPEAK FOR YOURSELF...

FANGPYRE

A Fangpyre bite gives everything a snakelike appearance—vehicles, Ninja, and even Jay's parents, Ed and Edna! Victims develop an inability to pronounce "s" words without a telltale hiss. The Fangpyre general, Fangtom, even grew an extra head when he bit himself by mistake.

FREE HUGS?

CONSTRICTAI

These powerful snakes torture their foes by wrapping their strong tails around their bodies. They can often be found deep underground, preparing for their next sneak attack, led by their brutish general, Skalidor.

"IT'S ABOUT TIME WE HAD A SERPENTINE BACK IN CHARGE."
SKALIDOR

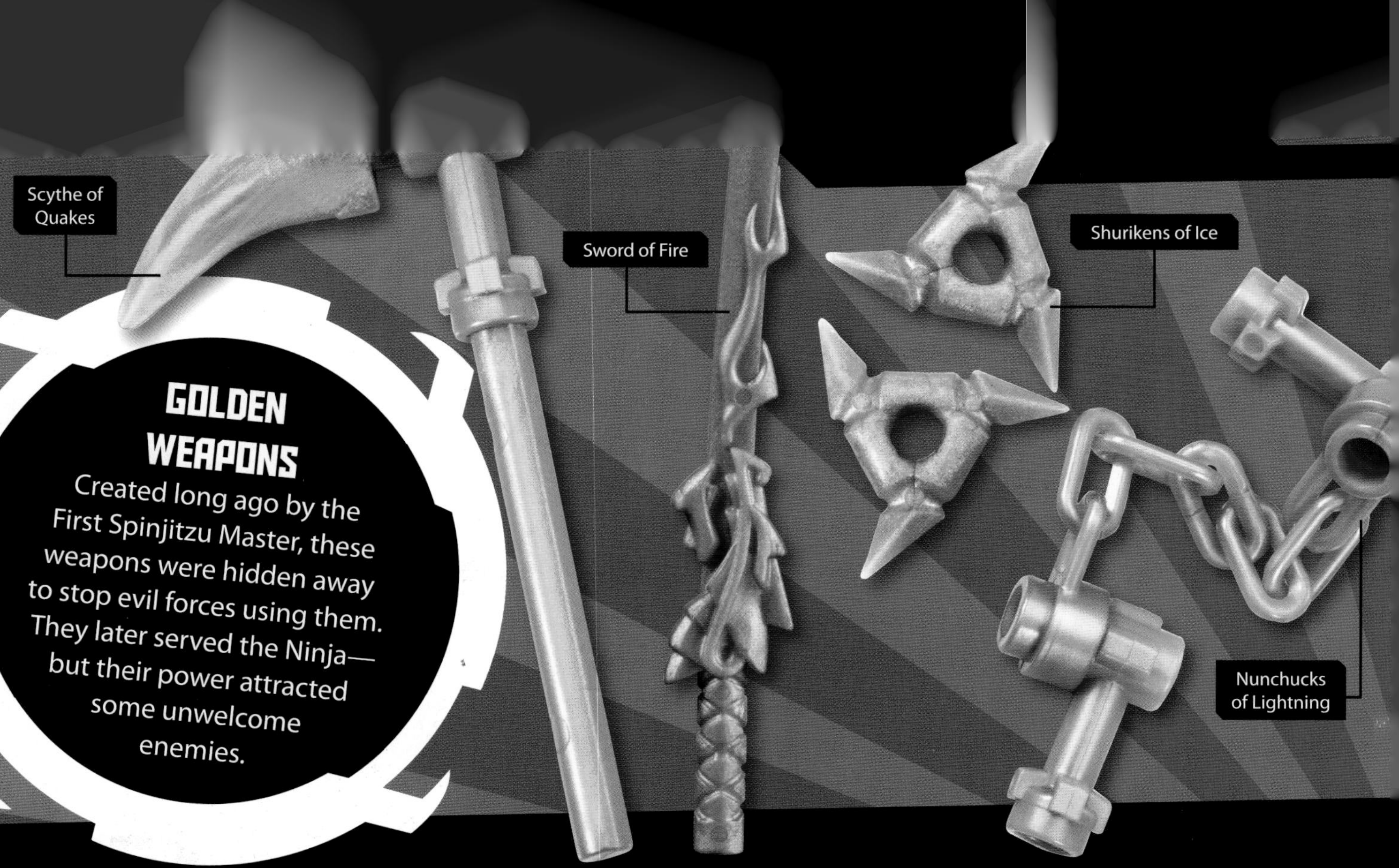

Scythe of
Quakes

Sword of Fire

Shurikens of Ice

GOLDEN WEAPONS

Created long ago by the
First Spinjitzu Master, these
weapons were hidden away
to stop evil forces using them.
They later served the Ninja—
but their power attracted
some unwelcome
enemies.

Nunchucks
of Lightning

THE POWER OF FOUR

Constrictai
Fang Blade

Hypnobrai
Fang Blade

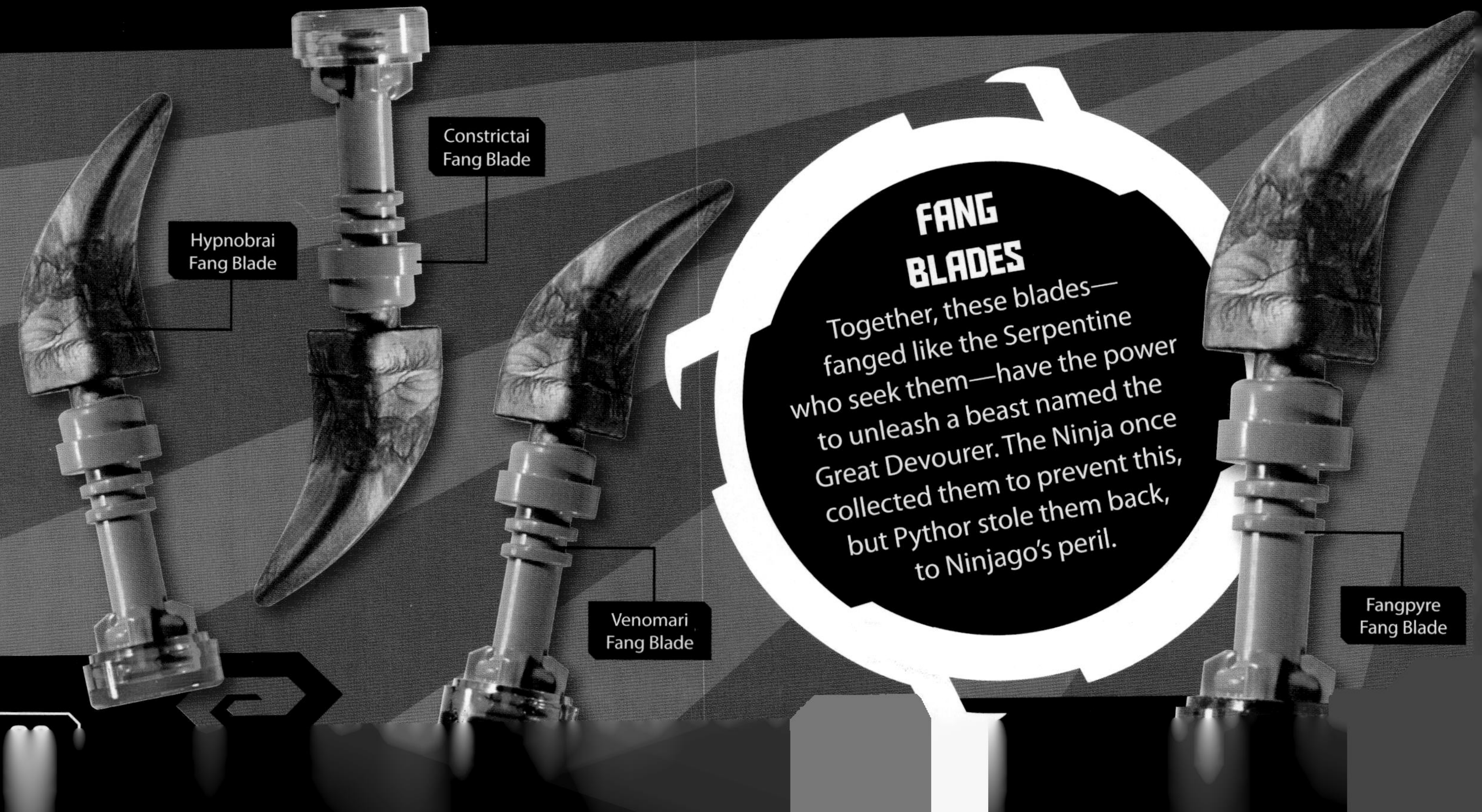

FANG BLADES

Together, these blades—
fanged like the Serpentine
who seek them—have the power
to unleash a beast named the
Great Devourer. The Ninja once
collected them to prevent this,
but Pythor stole them back,
to Ninjago's peril.

Venomari
Fang Blade

Fangpyre
Fang Blade

Jay's Elemental
Blade

Zane's Elemental
Blade

Cole's Elemental
Blade

ELEMENTAL BLADES

The blade of each weapon is formed by a burst of power that surges out from its golden hilt. Different for each Ninja, each blade strikes with the power of one of the elements: fire, earth, lightning, or ice.

Kai's Elemental
Blade

OUR ELEMENTS, four Ninja, and four f every awesome weapon—four certainly s a powerful number in Ninjago! Even some f the Ninja's enemies have realized the ower of this balanced number.

Jay's Techno
Blade

TECHNO BLADES

These blades are true "hackers"! They glow when they are near a computerized machine; the Ninja need only give the machine a whack to change its programming and transform it to their liking.

Kai's Techno
Blade

Cole's Techno
Blade

Zane's Techno
Blade

JAY'S PROFILE

📷 **POST A PICTURE**   ✉ **SEND A MESSAGE**   👥 **SEARCH FRIENDS**

Jay posted a picture

Jay Just got a new high score on Fist to Face 2! Don't be too jealous guys, we can't all have my lightning-fast reactions!
Ten minutes ago

Comments

Lloyd Whatever, Jay. Make way for the Green Ninja! I'll give it a try. Just let me at it.

Nya Are you seriously still playing that silly game? Don't you have training to do?

Kai You know I can beat you, Jay!

Jay posted a picture

Jay Fire and ice don't mix well on laundry day. Introducing... the Pink Ninja! Seven hours ago

No comments

Jay updated his location at **Master Chen's Noodle House**, with **Nya.** Yesterday at 18:30

Comments

Cole Bring home some egg rolls!

Zane posted a picture

Zane It took me a while to compute, but I think Sensei Wu could be dancing...
Two days ago

Comments

Nya Who knew Sensei had moves like that? Looking good, Wu!

Jay This had to be the funniest moment of the entire year! Sensei Wu making shapes on the dancefloor. Absolutely classic!

Jay posted a picture

Jay Step 1: Save the day. Step 2: Boogie all night at a victory party! Three days ago

Comments

 Zane Did someone say party? Computing optimal dance moves.

 Kai Yeah! Make way for the Ninja of Fire... 'cause my dance moves are smokin'!

 Cole If there's cake, I am IN.

 Nya It's party time!

Jay updated his status

Off to develop a few ideas in my workshop. I've had a flash of inspiration! Three days ago

Kai posted a picture of you

Kai The moment Cole got hit with a pie! Five days ago

Comments

 Cole Ha! I'm not the only funny thing in that picture. Check out Zane's apron!

 Zane What is so funny about my flowery apron?

 Jay Dude—are you serious?

 Zane An apron is an effective way to prevent food stains.

Jay posted a picture

Jay Check out the beach style: Awesome shorts, perfectly rumpled hair, just the right amount of blue. The best day EVER! Seven days ago

Comments

Zane When the weather is pleasant, a day on the beach is certainly most enjoyable.

 Cole Oh, man—do you hear yourself?

Kai This might have been a good moment for sunscreen... who knew I could get sunburned?

 Lloyd Sure, kick back while I'm off saving the world—no problem!

LLOYD

LIKE HIS FATHER, Garmadon, Lloyd knows what it's like to be the bad guy. But when he begins to learn of his true potential, Lloyd discovers powers he never knew he had—including the power to choose his own amazing path and become a hero.

HOME SWEET HOME

The Ninja used Spinjitzu to stop Lloyd's evil plans, but his uncle, Sensei Wu, knows what Lloyd really needs to mend his ways: a kind welcome, a caring home, and a bedtime story or two.

> I'VE REALLY GOT MY HANDS FULL!

"NINJA NEVER QUIT."
LLOYD

Golden armor deflects enemy blows

Decorative Green Ninja insignia

DATA FILE

- **Known for:** Being the chosen Green Ninja
- **Favorite weapon:** Golden katanas
- **Likes:** Comic books
- **Dislikes:** Having to train all the time

DESTINY REVEALED

Few thought that a kid like Lloyd could become the powerful Green Ninja. But to everyone's surprise, he is revealed as the fabled hero when the Golden Weapons emit a green glow in his presence.

MY DAD COULD BEAT YOURS IN A FIGHT.

TROUBLED YOUTH

Lloyd once dreamed of an evil career just like his dad. After running away from the School for Bad Boys, he did his devious best to stir up trouble—teaming up with venomous snakes and trying to steal all the candy in Ninjago!

Green robes match the bike perfectly

COMPACT CYCLE

Lloyd's green cycle is small, but seriously speedy! The Green Ninja hops on and stands behind the steering controls to drive, but the bike's two wide tires provide plenty of balance to help keep him upright!

Sturdy suspension for a smooth ride

DID YOU KNOW?

Lloyd once used a magical elixir to defeat a monster, but it also changed him from a kid to a grownup.

33

HOW DO YOU REACH YOUR TRUE POTENTIAL?

SENSEI WU SAYS "In each and every one of us there are obstacles that hold us back. Only when you conquer that fear will your heart be free." Lloyd struggles with this at first, but if his friends can overcome their obstacles, so can he.

FOLLOW YOUR OWN PATH

Cole unlocked his true potential by being honest with his father and telling him he wanted to be a Ninja, not a dancer. Once Cole felt confident about his own choices, he earned his dad's respect and some awesome new powers, too.

BE YOURSELF

Jay used to pretend that he was tougher, faster, or cooler than he really was—but Nya helped him realize that he didn't have to pretend: He is already the best version of himself, and that is enough.

SHARE YOUR STRENGTH

Kai was once so determined to be the best, he missed the chance to support his teammates. He found his true potential when he learned that he can succeed by helping others be their best.

ACCEPT YOUR PAST

Zane never knew where he came from, until he discovered the laboratory where he was built. Once he understood his origins, Zane was able to reach his true potential. He used his new powers to save his friends from harm.

DRAGON CARE

THINK YOU COULD take care of dragons for a day? The Ninja sometimes have to leave their dragons while they are off fighting enemies, but the dragons still need care and attention. A dragon sitter needs some inside info—and lots of courage—before taking on this fearsome foursome.

ROCKY

OWNER: Cole
ELEMENTAL POWER: Earth
DO: Give him his special dragon snack at 3pm.
DON'T: Forget his bedtime story!

SHARD

OWNER: Zane
ELEMENTAL POWER: Ice
DO: Offer him plenty of refreshing water.
DON'T: Let him get too hot.

FLAME

OWNER: Kai

ELEMENTAL POWER: Fire

DO: Let him out to fly at least once a day.

DON'T: Stand in front of him if he gets the hiccups.

WISP

OWNER: Jay

ELEMENTAL POWER: Lightning

DO: Pet him right between his eyes.

DON'T: Let him watch too much TV.

GREEN NINJA...
DRAGON SITTER?
THIS WAS NOT IN
THE SCROLLS!

NYA

SHE'S AN INVENTOR, navigator, and tech wiz—just not a Ninja. Sensei Wu did once ask Nya to join his dojo, but she is happy following her own path for now. She is still a key member of the team and often keeps the Ninja on track with her sensible advice.

DEFENDING HER TURF

Brave Nya never shies away from a challenge when her help is needed—like when she sails the Destiny Bounty through a terrifying storm! Nya's courage and skill prove she is every bit as tough as the boys.

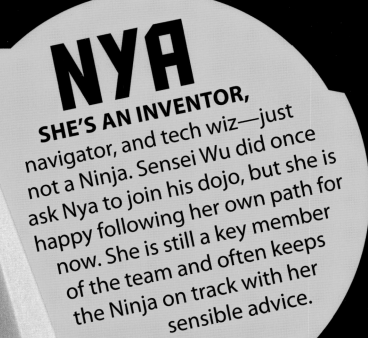

WATCH AND LEARN, BOYS!

"A GiRL'S GOT TO HAVE HER SECRETS!"
NYA

Trousers under Nya's dress allow her to race into action

Handheld daggers can be thrown at enemies

DATA FILE

- **Known for:** Amazing inventions
- **Favorite weapons:** Dagger and staff
- **Likes:** Cracking codes and solving mysteries
- **Dislikes:** Standing on the sidelines

SAMURAI BEATS NINJA EVERY TIME!

SECRET SAMURAI

While the Ninja are becoming famous in Ninjago, Nya trains in secret to become a powerful masked hero: Samurai X. Everyone is amazed at the power of the mysterious samurai, who can even outmaneuver the Ninja!

Mech even comes equipped with a cannon!

SAMURAI MECH

Her high-tech mech is just one of Nya's many cool inventions—but it sure is a showstopper! Towering over enemies, Nya can wield weapons, rescue allies, and even fly in this super-size armor.

DID YOU KNOW?

Although Nya appears to have inherited the same preference for red clothing as her brother Kai, her favorite color is blue... just like Jay's robes!

Phoenix symbol identifies the Samurai

ATTACK OF THE GREAT DEVOURER!

UNLEASHED BY THE Serpentine schemer Pythor, this mighty snake is on the loose in Ninjago City, eating everything in its path and getting larger and more terrifying by the bite. To stand a chance of defeating it, the Ninja will need quick thinking and great teamwork.

DID YOU KNOW?
This monster is the same tiny snake that bit Garmadon when he was a young boy.

STRIKE ONE...
Kai, Cole, Jay, and Zane try their best Spinjitzu moves, then they blast the tune of a Serpentine-slaying flute at the snake, but they still can't defeat this super-size creature.

STRIKE TWO...
In her big Mech, Nya is able to fly in and wedge the Devourer's mouth open. It's a good idea, but the dangerous maneuver doesn't stop the Devourer, and Nya nearly ends up inside its belly.

Underbelly of the snake is light green

STRIKE THREE!

The Ninja's dragons merge to form the Ultradragon—a four-headed beast with all their powers. Lloyd guides the Ultradragon toward the Great Devourer, but even a dragon can't overcome the greedy snake.

Powerful tail can sweep enemies off their feet

Red flame decoration represents Fire element

THE HUNGRY SNAKE

The Devourer eats everything in sight and grows bigger and bigger every second. It even thinks Pythor and Sensei Wu are a tasty snack! Luckily, it spits Wu and his teapot back out.

GARMADON... THE HERO?

The Devourer has a weak spot on its forehead, but the Ninja will have to trust their enemy, Garmadon, with their Golden Weapons if they hope to exploit it. With four arms, immense power, and a score to settle, he is the only one who can defeat the Devourer.

THE HISTORY OF THE OVERLORD

LONG BEFORE TIME had a name, at the very creation of Ninjago itself, there was good and there was evil—and there is no one more evil than a spirit named the Overlord. Here is his story...

BEGINNINGS

A legendary warrior named the First Spinjitzu Master used the four Golden Weapons to create the land known today as Ninjago.

A PEACEFUL LAND

The First Spinjitzu Master created Ninjago as a peaceful and bountiful land of light. But wherever there is light, there must also be shadow...

DARKNESS LURKS

Out of the shadows, the Overlord was born—shaped by the darkness and born to counterbalance goodness and light.

FIERCE FOES

For many years, the evil, shadowy Overlord menaced the people of Ninjago. The First Spinjitzu Master worked tirelessly to keep the danger at bay, but the Overlord grew stronger—despite his lack of physical form.

MASTER PLAN

Eventually, the Overlord concocted his most terrifying plan yet. He used his powers to bring to life a number of powerful stone warriors.

THE STONE ARMY RISES

Hungry for power, the Overlord used his Stone Army to challenge the First Spinjitzu Master for control of Ninjago.

A BATTLE RAGES

The First Spinjitzu Master fought bravely against the Overlord and his immense army, but could not destroy his enemy.

A DIFFICULT CHOICE

As the Stone Army overwhelmed him, the First Spinjitzu Master was forced to plunge his sword into the ground and split Ninjago into two.

THE LAND DIVIDES

Ninjago was split into two halves: darkness and light. The Overlord was banished to the Dark Island, which sunk beneath the sea, and Ninjago regained its peaceful existence.

THE STONE ARMY

ANCIENT AND INDESTRUCTIBLE, the Stone Army was created by the Overlord for his fight against the First Spinjitzu Master. Luckily for Ninjago, they were then buried deep beneath the earth. Now they have awoken to terrorize the city once more.

CAN WE PLAY MUSICAL STATUES?

WARRIOR
It is hard to say what is scariest about these stone warriors: their huge helmets or creepy face markings. These fearsome fighters report directly to their general.

SWORDSMAN
The majority of the Stone Army is formed of loyal swordsmen, armed with katanas and conical hats. With endless stamina, these stone figures never stand still for very long.

SCOUT
The scouts make up the lowest rank in the Stone Army. These sneaky characters are expected to be nimble, fast, and remain out of sight when hunting their enemies.

GENERAL KOZU
General Kozu towers over the other stone warriors with his large helmet and extra set of arms. He translates the warrior's ancient language for the Overlord.

LIVING STATUE

Lloyd's mother, Misako, works in Ninjago City's museum, home to a relic of a giant stone warrior. But when venom from the Great Devourer touches the ancient artifact, it comes to life and quickly resumes its task of destruction.

UNBEATABLE STRENGTH

The tough Stone Army are powered by Dark Matter, which make them indestructible so they can withstand fierce attacks. The Ninja will have tough job trying to stop them!

DID YOU KNOW?
The Stone Army kidnapped an inventor called Dr. Julien and forced him to create weapons and vehicles to use against their enemies.

Samurai horns

Sharp side spikes

Single tread at front of vehicle

WARRIOR BIKE

The Stone Army have many weapons and vehicles at their disposal, including this fearsome machine. They use the Warrior Bike to tear around the Dark Island seeking out enemies and attacking intruders.

COLE

THIS TOUGH GUY can lift heavy loads, throw massive objects, and lead his fellow Ninja through just about anything. But Cole, Ninja of Earth, is at his most powerful when he learns to mix his incredible strength with flexibility, an open mind, and some killer dance moves.

MUSCLE MAN

Some may like to lift weights, but with Cole's astonishing rock-hard muscles he can hoist a couple of friends—and their dinner—into the air! Cole is the strongest of the four Ninja, and can carry out amazing feats of strength.

"STAY STRONG. SHOW NO WEAKNESS.
COLE

Green Techno Blade is an unusual splash of color for Cole

DATA FILE

- ✵ **Known for:**
  Strength and dependability
- ✕ **Favorite weapon:**
  Scythe of Quakes
- 👍 **Likes:**
  Mountain climbing
- 👎 **Dislikes:**
  Disloyalty and snakes

Chain attached to blade's hilt can be used as a weapon

ROCKY AND COLE

Cole can't stand dragons—or at least that's what he thought until he had one of his own. With Earth Dragon Rocky, Cole is like a doting dad: showering his beloved dragon with affection and snacks, and even ordering him special treats in the mail.

Drill is powered by a powerful motor

EARTH DRILLER

Sensible Cole is always down-to-earth, but in his Earth Driller he even powers through it! The giant drill on the front of his vehicle can tunnel through immense obstacles. Despite its size, the speedy Driller can still leave enemies spluttering in its dusty tracks.

DID YOU KNOW?
Cole is a dance champ! His signature move is the Triple Tiger Sashay—a tricky aerial feat that amazes dance fans (including Cole's dad).

CAN YOU SURVIVE THE DARK ISLAND?

COLE KNOWS IT won't be easy to attack the Overlord's Dark Island Base —there are dangers everywhere. But if the Ninja stick together, stay hidden, and use all their skills, they should be able to defeat the Overlord and escape.

AVOID EVIL

SCOUT THE ENEMY CAMP

The Overlord senses when enemies are near, and sends the Stone Army to imprison them. Try not to become an unwilling test subject for his plan to infect Ninjago with Dark Matter. He has already corrupted Nya with evil, and she is trouble enough!

New elemental powers can be found in the Temple of Light —but you'll have to figure out on your own how to unlock them. Fortunately there seems to be some clues in the Temple, and four convenient spaces to place weapons…

The stone warriors speak an ancient language almost no one can understand. But by watching their movements, it's possible to see what they are up to—digging up evil Dark Matter and building the Overlord's Ultimate Weapon. Just don't get caught!

RECEIVE YOUR POWERS

BEWARE THE GARMATRON

Once the immense Garmatron is loaded up with Dark Matter, it can infect anyone with evil in a single shot. Steer clear of this dangerous machine—if you are unfortunate enough to meet it, run away as fast as you can!

RACE TO NINJAGO!

IF THEY ARE to have any hope of returning to Ninjago City and defeating the Overlord, the Ninja must first find the Temple of Light, unite the Elemental Swords, and activate the First Spinjitzu Master's Golden Mech. No problem!

Stacked roof in the traditional Ninjago style

DID YOU KNOW?

Lloyd's mother, Misako, advises the Ninja to find the Temple of Light. She has heard ancient myths detailing its power.

FAR TO GO

Lloyd's leg is injured and the Ninja have given away their elemental powers. It seems impossible the team of heroes will be able to cross the vast ocean that stands between them and Ninjago City.

Murals show Ninjago's ancient masters

Weapons rack

HOME AT LAST

Revived by the Golden Ninja, the Golden Mech works like an enormous suit of armor, battle tank, and robot warrior all rolled into one. Despite his injury, Lloyd is able to fly the Mech back to Ninjago to face the Overlord. The rest of the gang follow on the Ultradragon to witness the epic showdown.

Gleaming golden armor

TEMPLE OF LIGHT

The Temple of Light looks like a peaceful palace— but as the hiding place of the Elemental Blades and Golden Mech, it holds incredible power. A few Stone Army warriors won't keep Lloyd from uncovering his destiny within its ancient walls.

THE GOLDEN NINJA

LLOYD IS BACK from the Dark Island, and he is raring to use his new Golden Ninja powers. The Overlord is planning on spreading evil and darkness across Ninjago, but Lloyd won't let that happen without a fight!

Lloyd rides a Golden Dragon, summoned using his new powers

Green face detail matches the detail

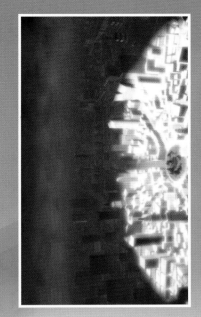

GOLDEN BOY

No ordinary weapon can defeat the Overlord. Lloyd uses his new powers to conjure a spinning ball of light and summon a magical Golden Dragon to help destroy the villain.

Pure gold shoulder armor

ENDLESS ARMY

The Ninja are hopelessly outnumbered as the vast Stone Army closes in on them. They are relying on Lloyd's new powers to save Ninjago... but will he be strong enough?

LIGHT RETURNS

Lloyd is victorious! Defeating the Overlord causes the evil that had infected Ninjago to disperse. The dark shadows lift and all is well again.

Even Lloyd's hands are awash with golden energy

GOOD GARMADON

As light returns to Ninjago, those corrupted by evil are cured. Lloyd gets a reward more valuable than gold—the return of his father. Without evil, Garmadon is once again simply Lloyd's dad. He is unrecognizable!

ZANE

WITH A MYSTERIOUS past and some odd ways, Zane has always been a little different. But there is more to this Ninja than even his closest friends suspect. Inside, he is a robot! His fellow Ninja still consider Zane a true brother, despite his high-tech circuitry.

SNACK TIME

When raiding the fridge for a midnight snack, only Zane climbs right in to eat his sandwich on the top shelf! The cold isn't a problem for the Ninja of Ice. But for his fellow Ninja, it can be a shock to find their friend sitting next to the cheese.

"IT'S ICE TO SEE YOU."
ZANE

Zane's Techno Blade glows icy blue when powered up

DATA FILE

✷ **Known for:**
Oddball ways

✖ **Favorite weapon:**
Shurikens of Ice

👍 **Likes:**
Cold hard facts

👎 **Dislikes:**
Rusty joints

DID YOU KNOW?
Nindroid Zane can record sound, figure out the odds of victory, and stay underwater for more than ten minutes.

Snowy white robes never get dirty

FUNNY MAN?

When ultra-serious Zane discovered the switch that reactivated his memory, he also found a way to switch on his sense of humor—and launched into a hilarious song-and-dance routine!

> LOGICALLY, I AM THE COOLEST OF THE NINJA.

FALCON FRIEND

Master inventor Dr. Julien built Zane and his trusty mechanical falcon. This robotic bird becomes a trusted friend and guide. Zane can even tap into the falcon's vision to see distant enemies.

SPEEDING SNOWMOBILE

When he learns to focus his elemental power, Zane can create this machine out of thin air. With the Ninja of Ice on its back, the powerful snowmobile speeds across the snow, shooting enemies with devastating blasts of ice.

Icicle decorations match Zane's frosty powers

BUILDING ZANE

AN ADVANCED MACHINE like Zane takes plenty of planning, a good dose of tinkering, and a brilliant mind like Dr. Julien's to bring it all to life.

NINJA MASK
Dr. Julien could have included a built-in mask—but this removable design lets Zane keep a more human appearance.

OCULAR PROCESSOR
Regular people would call this an eye—but the instrument Zane uses to see can also record, scan, and analyze just like a computer.

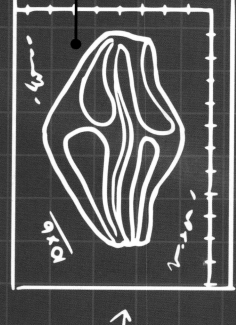

CIRCUITS AND SWITCHES

A hinged door in Zane's chest makes it easy to access his inner workings. Inside are a number of switches that control Zane's programming.

CONTROL PANEL

All Zane needs to do to quickly access his settings is flip open his sleeve and—tada!—a switchboard. Perfect for a mid-battle upgrade!

HEAD TO TOE

Zane is unusual in many ways but with his standard head-to-toe measurement, he is exactly the same height as the other Ninja.

DEFAULT SETTINGS

POWER SOURCE:	EXTENSION CORD	☒	SENSE OF HUMOR:	ON	☒	OPTIONAL ABILITIES:	BREATHING UNDERWATER	☑
	BATTERY	☒		OFF	☑		FLIGHT	☒
	ENHANCED CORE	☑	SINGING ABILITY:	ON	☒		DANCE SKILLS	☑
MEMORY:	ON	☒		OFF	☑		GENEROSITY	☑
	OFF	☑	FRIENDSHIP FUNCTION:	ON	☑		FIGHTING SKILL	☑
				OFF	☒		FASHION SENSE	☒

P.I.X.A.L.

WHAT DOES GENIUS Ninjago inventor, Cyrus Borg, do when he needs the perfect assistant? He builds one, of course! The result: a completely personalized Nindroid named Primary Interactive X-ternal Assistant Life-form—or P.I.X.A.L. for short.

SWEET 16

The P.I.X.A.L. we know wasn't the first: It took 16 tries for Cyrus to work out some of her design kinks, including an emotion suppressor that's still not quite perfect.

> HOW CAN I BE OF ASSISTANCE?

"I AM NOT BUILT FOR STEALTH.
P.I.X.A.L.

DATA FILE

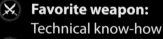

- **Known for:** Analytical abilities
- **Favorite weapon:** Technical know-how
- **Likes:** Being helpful—especially to Zane!
- **Dislikes:** Computer malfunctions

Exposed circuitry is visible under purple robes

COMPUTER GIRL

P.I.X.A.L. has amazing computing abilities—she can calculate huge sums, access endless facts, and make logical, data-based choices. P.I.X.A.L.'s programming also determines whether she is good or bad. She has cheerful green eyes when she is good, but watch out when they switch to red!

NINJA ALLY

P.I.X.A.L. is built to be helpful—and when her friends the Ninja are under attack, she does what she can to help. She knows she is not built for battle, but she has a few moves!

DID YOU KNOW?

P.I.X.A.L.'s programming means that computer viruses and power outages can cause her to glitch or shut down completely.

Central spinning rotor provides lift

P.I.X.A.L. sits in the front seat

PERFECT CO-PILOT

P.I.X.A.L. puts her amazing skills to good use when helping pilot Zane's Ninjacopter. With Zane at the controls, P.I.X.A.L. keeps careful watch over the flashing control panel.

THE NINDROIDS

INITIATE ATTACK!

THE OVERLORD IS BACK—and he is digital! The Digital Overlord has infected the computer systems that control New Ninjago City and with the help of a robot army, he is planning a technological takeover. His Nindroids are based on Zane's blueprints, but they've been upgraded with increased speed and strength.

GENERAL CRYPTOR

The Nindroid general is heavily armored, with two katanas and advanced programming. In command of the vast Nindroid army and their vehicles and weapons, he enforces the Digital Overlord's orders.

WARRIORS

Nindroid warriors don't need emotions to know where their loyalties lie: They'll follow General Cryptor's orders to their last spark of energy.

DRONES

Drones have very simple programming, so they follow orders without thinking and never lose focus on their mission.

MINDROID

The smallest of the Nindroids, Mindroid is constantly teased by his fellow fighters. This pint-sized fighter has a big point to prove.

CYRUS BORG

Once a force for peace and progress in New Ninjago City, inventor Cyrus Borg has been forced into the service of the Digital Overlord. Borg's own technology was turned against him to modify its kindly creator into a war machine. Borg warned the Ninja about the Overlord before his transformation, but they can't rely on his help now!

DESTRUCTOID

The name says it all! This Nindroid vehicle is mechanized mayhem. Rolling tracks to go over any terrain, front blasters, an extendable rotating saw, a massive sword and shield—everything about this machine spells trouble.

DID YOU KNOW?
The Nindroids are based on Zane's blueprints, but they don't contain his unique internal energy source. They rely on external power, so power cuts are bad news for Nindroids!

Saw blade

Moving mech arm

Chopping front blade

61

THE PERFECT MATCH MACHINE

WHEN THE NINJA visit Borg Industries with the students of Wu's new academy, Nya accompanies them. Her students persuade her to try the Perfect Match Machine, which can predict your soulmate.

SURPRISE MATCH
Nya is shocked when the Perfect Match Machine suggests Cole is her ideal date, rather than Jay!

JAY AND NYA

RATING: COMPATIBLE

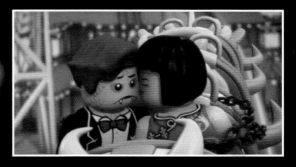

Not a perfect match, but very strong compatibility. These two cool characters bring out the best in each other.

NYA AND COLE

RATING: PERFECT MATCH

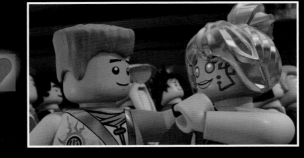

An ideal pairing! Common areas include strength, thoughtfulness, and temperament.

MISAKO AND WU

RATING: EXCELLENT

A true meeting of minds makes this an outstanding match. Obstacles stand in the way of a relationship however.

ZANE AND P.I.X.A.L.

RATING: COMPATIBLE

With slight modifications, a perfect match can be achieved. Programming and settings are compatible.

KAI AND SKYLOR

RATING: UNCERTAIN

Sparks of romance exist, but without trust the relationship cannot develop further.

WHAT CAN THE NINJA HACK?

CYRUS BORG GAVE the Ninja the Techno Blades to help them reprogramme the evil infecting Ninjago. But the blades also help them make some serious upgrades.

THUNDER RAIDER

With mighty tank treads and rugged tires, Jay's transformed ride storms over rough ground at lightning speeds. For a truly powerful partnership, Cole's Earth Mech can attach to the back to add horsepower and firepower.

EARTH MECH

Cole pounds the ground with each giant step in his fearsome Earth Mech. With built-in missile launchers and stunning speed, the Earth Mech can run, climb, and even join forces with Jay for a team machine that can't be beat.

KAI FIGHTER

An ordinary vehicle becomes this awesome aircraft with a touch of Kai's Techno Blade. In it, Kai can take flight in a blur of red, launching missiles at his enemies as he engages super-speed mode to escape enemy blasts.

NINJACOPTER

Zane flies high in this teched-out copter that's as smooth as ice. Hacked with his Techno Blade, it slices through the air to fight off Nindroids and defend the people of Ninjago.

SENSEI GARMADON

After he is cured of the evil that possessed him, the once-wicked Garmadon finds a new, peaceful path. At his remote monastery, Sensei Garmadon teaches the Ninja to use speed and stealth to outwit enemies—without turning to weapons or violence.

ALLY OR

IN NINJAGO, THE LINES between good and evil can sometimes get a littl blurred. Just ask these two brothers— they know that good guys and bad guys aren't always what they seem!

"THE KEY IS BALANCE."
SENSEI GARMADON

"HE'S TURNED EVIL. HELP ME!"
KAI

ENEMY?

TECH WU
Only the Digital Overlord could have retooled gentle Sensei Wu into this mean metal fighting machine! Tech Wu has all of the Sensei's skills, corrupted with a dark new mission: Help the Overlord and destroy the Ninja.

THE MIGHTY MECHDRAGON ATTACKS!

THE DIGITAL OVERLORD is determined to get his (virtual) hands on Lloyd. He believes that harnessing Lloyd's golden powers will give him the physical form he desires. The Overlord sends Tech Wu and the enormous MechDragon to track him down.

Samurai flag

PEACEFUL POP

After he becomes good again, Sensei Garmadon is eager to make up for lost time with his son. When Lloyd is forced to hide from the Digital Overlord, his father joins him for support. Garmadon tries to pass on some of his wisdom on their father-son roadtrip!

WINGED NINDROID

The MechDragon is crammed full of the most up-to-date technology available in New Ninjago City. The Digital Overlord has complete control over its spinning blade wheels and razor-sharp wings—bad news for Lloyd and Sensei Garmadon!

Nindroid controls cannon

Traditional cannon has had a high-tech makeover

Metal claws

DRIVING DUO

Lloyd and his father have to get away fast in an armored vehicle when they encounter the MechDragon. Sensei Garmadon steers while Lloyd mans the vehicle's missile launcher. Garmadon has made a vow of peace, but facing this fearsome foe is a real test of wills.

OUT OF LUCK?

Lloyd and his father manage to outrun the MechDragon once, but it soon returns to strike again. This time, Lloyd is captured while trying to save his father. A robotic snake binds his arms together and he is carried off to be delivered to the Overlord.

WHAT HAPPENS IN THE DIGIVERSE?

THANKS TO ONE of Cyrus Borg's inventions, and some technical support from P.I.X.A.L., it is possible for the Ninja to enter the digital realm where the Digital Overlord is residing. Their mission: fight and defeat the Overlord before he regains his physical form.

TECH WORLD

Inside the Digiverse, regular rules don't apply. Instead, it's as if the Ninja are characters in a video game—an idea that's thrilling to tech-fan Jay and simply terrifying to Kai. Not a gadget fan, Kai struggles to control his new powers.

IMAGINATION RULES

To cope with the ever-changing rules in the Digiverse, the Ninja must imagine the powers they need: jumping huge distances, turning upside-down, and creating vehicles out of thin air.

DID YOU KNOW?
When the Ninja wipe the Overlord from the Digiverse, Wu is no longer corrupted by evil technology. He returns to his normal self and stretches out a friendly hand to his brother.

LIGHT IN DARKNESS

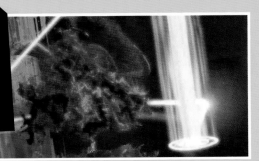

When the Digital Overlord blocks their path, the Ninja must find a way to surround him with the light of their Techno Blades. They use their minds to connect their beams and destroy the heart of the Overlord's digital system.

MEANWHILE...

While the Ninja fight in the digital world, Nya and P.I.X.A.L. take on the Nindroids in Borg Tower—struggling to protect the technology that will let the Ninja return to the real world. Wu once again battles his brother, but this time it is Sensei Garmadon protecting the Ninja!

THE ODDS OF SUCCESS ARE TOO SLIM TO CALCULATE...

THAT HAS NEVER STOPPED US BEFORE!

CAN YOU REALLY TRUST A SNAKE?

IN EVERY BEING, there is both good and evil—look at Sensei Garmadon! The slithering Serpentine have also been viewed as evil for many long years—but from their point of view, things are very different.

SHEDDING OLD SKINS

In their underground dwelling, the Serpentine have turned over a new leaf—taking lessons in good manners and educating their young about the stories they hold dear. In their way, they are trying to be unified, helpful, and good.

THE HEROES OF NINJAGO

In their legends, the Serpentine tell their children of their efforts to save the world from the evil they know is coming. When they tried to warn the humans, they were attacked and driven underground. To a loving father like Scales, being treated as evil seems a great injustice.

The Serpentine believe that a Golden Master will overturn all that is good in Ninjago, bringing about a new age of evil that cannot be defeated. Could they be mistaking the Golden Ninja for the evil Golden Master?

THE CURSE OF THE GOLDEN MASTER

DID YOU KNOW?

The Ninja believed Pythor was lost forever in the stomach of the Great Devourer. Pythor actually escaped, although the acid in the monster's belly bleached his purple scales to white.

A SNAKE AMONG SNAKES

The Ninja consult the snakes when a mysterious enemy leaves behind a white scale after a battle. They believe that the individual is working for the Digital Overlord, and is using Electrocobrai —underwater snakes that carry electricity—to power the Nindroids. The Serpentine know Pythor is the only snake capable of such mischief.

X-1 NINJA CHARGER

NINJA ARE TRAINED in stealth—but with a car like this, Kai prefers racing down the highway and getting plenty of attention. This speedster is packed with technical gadgets and a computer system that keeps him in touch with his team.

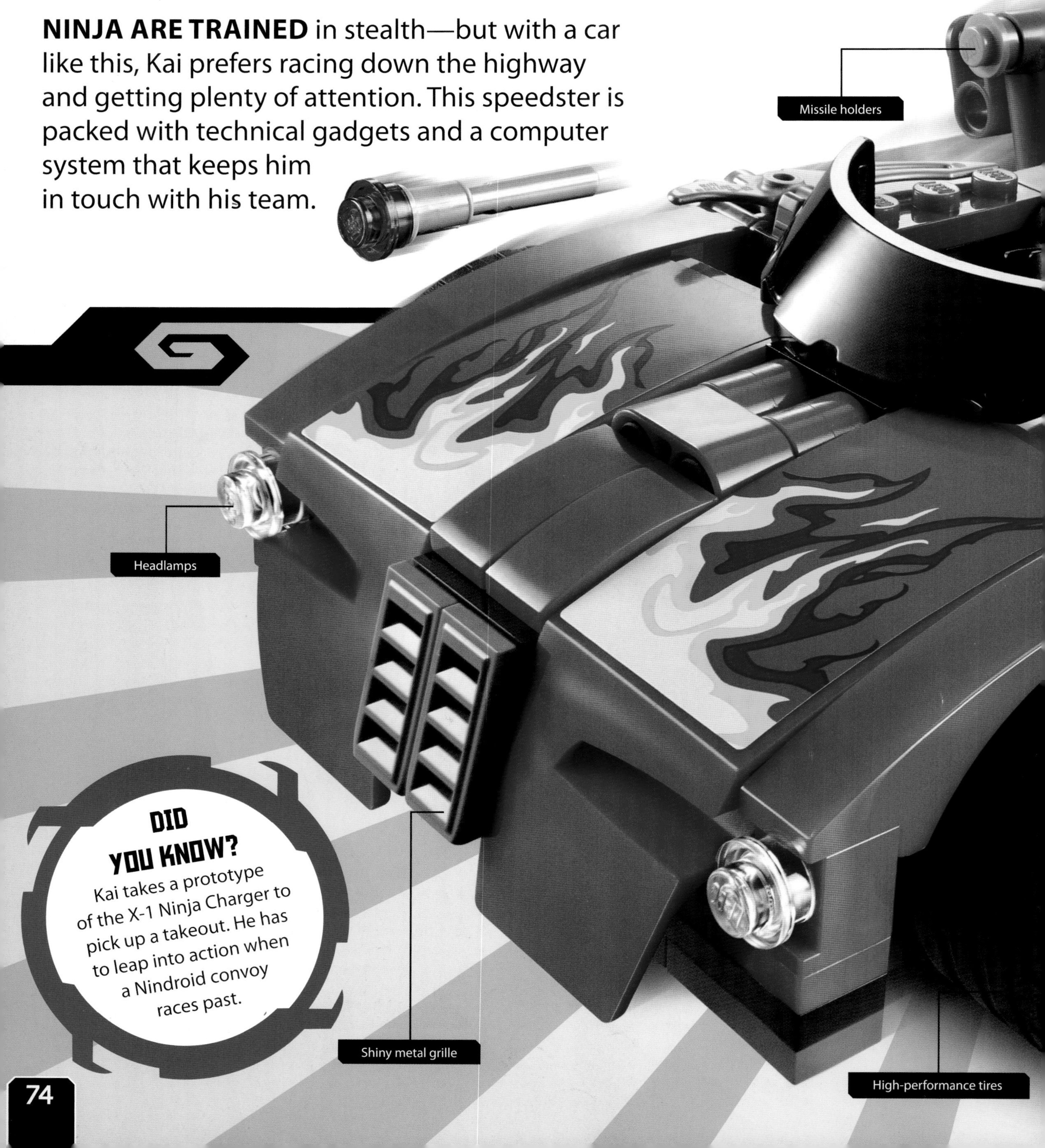

Missile holders

Headlamps

DID YOU KNOW?
Kai takes a prototype of the X-1 Ninja Charger to pick up a takeout. He has to leap into action when a Nindroid convoy races past.

Shiny metal grille

High-performance tires

Golden detail

Exposed engine

Spoiler stops drag
slowing the car down

DID YOU KNOW?
P.I.X.A.L. passes mission details to Kai through the X-1 Ninja Charger's radio system. She can even drive the car remotely.

Golden wheel rims

Wheel spokes cover
hidden weapons

Side panels are
aerodynamically designed

INTERCEPTOR BIKE
Sometimes Kai is in a tight spot and needs a more compact ride to chase after an enemy. Never fear—the X-1 Ninja Charger has a detachable motorcycle with matching flame details.

DEFEND AGAINST THE OVERLORD!

Zane's jetpack

THE WORST HAS happened—the Digital Overlord has gained a physical form and become the fabled Golden Master. He has all of Ninjago in his evil control. Can the Ninja defeat him before all hope is lost?

The Overlord's flesh form

TRAPPED NINJA

Even fighting as one, the Ninja are no match for the vast power of the Golden Master, whose golden web of power stretches across New Ninjago City.

LARGE AND IN CHARGE

After a long quest to regain a physical form, the Overlord has a physical body and more—his maniacal Mech gives him terrifying powers and abilities.

Robotic foreleg

TEMPLE OF FORTITUDE

This strong temple offers cool new armored robes for Zane, and temporary protection for the Ninja—until the Nindroids arriv[e]

ZANE'S SACRIFICE

To save his fellow Ninja, Zane sacrifices himself—plugging himself into the web and absorbing the frightful power of the Golden Master to defeat the Digital Overlord. The Ninja are devasted at the loss of their brother.

Zip wire provides a speedy descent

Stone staircase

THE TOURNAMENT OF ELEMENTS

CALLING ALL HEROES OF NINJAGO!

Do you have what it takes to come out on top?

Find out at Master Chen's **TOURNAMENT OF ELEMENTS!**

Take part in the event of the year—pitting power against power, and hero against hero, in a historic fight for glory!

WHEN: THIS WEEK
WHERE: MASTER CHEN'S ISLAND

MASTER CHEN

THE PEOPLE OF NINJAGO know Master Chen as the face of their favorite chain of noodle restaurants. But behind his cheerful front, he's really a scheming master criminal, out to steal the Ninja's powers and unleash chaos on Ninjago.

NOODLE HOUSE

What could be more innocent than a delicious dinner? Master Chen's restaurants are known for tasty bowls of noodles and the giant winking Chen sign above the door. His customers don't know about Chen's devious plans to take over Ninjago.

> FORGET NOODLES, WANT POWER

DATA FILE

- **Known for:** His chain of Noodle House restaurants
- **Favorite weapon:** The Staff of Elements
- **Likes:** Power and deceit
- **Dislikes:** Anyone who wants to stand in his way

"I HOLD ALL THE CARDS!"
MASTER CHEN

I'LL KEEP AN EYE OUT.

DADDY'S GIRL?

Chen's daughter, Skylor, is used to her father's trickery and schemes, so it is no surprise when he orders her to spy on the Ninja. But there's more to Skylor than following orders: She has the ability to absorb the powers of others—and maybe even to make some powerful choices of her own.

STAFF OF ELEMENTS

Master Chen's staff was made from crystals from the caves of his secret island. Each time a contestant in his tournament is defeated, the staff can collect the fighter's powers, making it even more powerful—and dangerous—with every battle.

Bulky build isn't sleek, but it is strong

ANACONDRAI COPTER

Chen has spent years building his army, including some Anacondrai equipment sure to have enemies on the run: This Serpentine flyer packs some frightening firepower, and lets Chen enjoy all the mayhem from high in the air.

DID YOU KNOW?
The noodles in Chen's restaurants are made by imprisoned workers on his secret island.

WHO ARE THE ELEMENTAL MASTERS?

A NUMBER OF Elemental Masters have arrived to compete in the Tournament of Elements, but the Ninja suspect one of them is a traitor. Nya goes undercover to help the Ninja get the lowdown on all the crazy competitors.

SHADE
MASTER OF SHADOW
Suspicious Shade stays out of the limelight, always nervous that others are out to get him.

JACOB
MASTER OF SOUND
Blind fighter Jacob can't see what's in front of him, but you'd be surprised what his other senses can tell him.

SKYLOR
MASTER OF ABSORBTION
Skylor can absorb the powers of other fighters—a serious threat considering the company she keeps.

MR. PALE
MASTER OF LIGHT
The power to bend and control light makes it impossible to see Mr. Pale if he doesn't want you to.

ASH
MASTER OF SMOKE
You can't pin down Ash— as soon as anyone gets too close, he disappears in a puff of smoke!

TOX
MASTER OF POISON

This venomous competitor is ready with a dose of poison for anyone who seems like a threat.

KARLOF
MASTER OF METAL

A big brute with a loyal heart, Karlof has fists of steel... and he's not afraid to use them.

TRY HEAVY METAL.

CHAMILLE
MASTER OF FORM

The mysterious master is hard to spot—just when you think you know what she looks like, she changes form again!

BOLOBO
MASTER OF NATURE

Powerful but worn from age, this old fighter has the power to control nature.

NEURO
MASTER OF MIND

The ability to read thoughts makes Neuro a dangerous foe—but also a nervous one.

GRAVIS
MASTER OF GRAVITY

Anyone fighting Gravis will soon feel their world turn upside-down as he twists and turns gravity itself.

I JUST NEED SOME RUNNING MUSIC!

GRIFFIN TURNER
MASTER OF SPEED

He's not one to wait around for anything—fun-loving Griffin is always rushing to the scene of the action.

THE ANACONDRA

MASTER CHEN
Master Chen has one dream: to become one with the Anacondrai and begin a new reign of terror in Ninjago! Each of his followers has a purple snake tattoo to show their loyalty to Chen and his cause.

OF ALL THE slithery snakes in Ninjago one tribe is the most dangerous. Known as the fiercest fighters in Serpentine history, the Anacondrai were banished to the Underworld long ago—but if Master Chen has his way, they'll soon be back!

> I'VE GOT A FANGTASTIC PLAN

CLOUSE
Chen's second in command, Clouse, used to be Garmadon's training partner—but only Garmadon achieved the title of Lord. Now Clouse wants to get revenge on Garmadon for outshining him all those years ago.

ZUGU
Zugu is the perfect guard for Master Chen's underground noodle factory: He's tough, willing to follow orders without question, and will do anything for food!

EYEZOR
He has just one working eye—but Eyezor can spot ways to create mayhem wherever he looks. Mean, mohawked, and dead-set on making his enemies suffer, Eyezor is the perfect sidekick for Chen's destructive plans.

CHOPE-CHOPE
Chope-Chope invented his own name to seem menacing—although some would say his scary grimace and ruthless fighting style are quite enough for that!

KAPAU

"SCALE IT DOWN, BUDDY"

Like Chope-Chope, Kapau renamed himself to sound tough and scary. Their plan worked—both friends are rising in the ranks of Chen's army, whether or not their skills deserve it.

SLEVEN

Sleven is more than willing to go along with Chen's plans to take on Anacondrai powers. This slithery guy already acts like a snake, he just needs a tail to complete his image!

KRAIT

As a loyal footsoldier in Chen's Army, Krait is dedicated to squashing Chen's enemies, helping steal the Elemental Masters' powers, and completing the army's Anacondrai transformation—no questions asked.

PYTHOR

Pythor is a true Anacondrai—vital to Chen's plan of transforming his army into snake-like warriors. His misadventures have left him bleached white, but his devious mind is still full of colorful plans.

Anacondrai warrior sword

Spinning blade rotors

Tribal printing on wheels

ANACONDRAI CRUSHER

This Anacondrai Crusher has massive jaws—making it a frightening sight to anyone who crosses its path. It has spinning blades, a slashing tail, striking speed, and its bite is just as deadly as it looks.

HERO'S HONOR
The Ninja last saw Zane in battle, when his brave actions overpowered the Overlord—but also overloaded his own circuits. This statue of Zane was built in Ninjago, in his memory.

DID YOU KNOW?
Zane was captured by Master Chen while trying to find his fellow Ninja. After his own capture, Cole is the first Ninja to discover Zane 2.0.

ZANE SACRIFICED HIMSELF during the battle against the Overlord. His Ninja friends never gave up hope they would see him again... but they never expected this rebooted new version!

Characters mean "dragon"

CE DRAGON

ocked away in Chen's
rison, Zane is haunted
y a terrifying dragon in his
reams. Zane soon realises
e must face his fear to
arness the dragon's power.

神龍

Rider's mount

Icy scales

ZANE PXL

P.I.X.A.L.'s physical form is gone, but when Zane downloads her operating system it is as if the two friends are merged in a single titanium body.

NINJA VS. SNAKES!

Handheld sai weapon

IT FEELS LIKE this has all happened before—but this new gang of snakes is a whole new threat. Master Chen is building his own Anacondrai army at a temple hidden on his secret island. He plans to start a new Serpentine War and take control of Ninjago.

LOOKALIKES

Pythor used to be the only one of his species, but not any more. It turns out members of the tribe all have similar traits: purple skin, red eyes, and an unnerving ability to swallow people whole.

ANACONDRAI TEMPLE

Chen takes over this ancient abandoned temple and uses is as the base for his growing snake army. It shows his admiration for the Anacondrai—this was the tribe's own temple many, many years ago.

Serpent head

Fangs

WATCHFUL LEADER
Clutching his powerful staff, Chen oversees the battle—ready to soak up the powers of any fallen fighters.

RETURN OF THE SNAKES
Chen is obsessed with the Anacondrai and is determined to transform his army into the powerful snakes. All it takes is an ancient spell book, Clouse's magical abilities, the stolen elemental powers, and the help of Pythor!

THREATS TO NINJAGO

THE NINJA HAVE battled so many enemies, sometimes it's tough to keep track of them all—especially when they keep switching sides! It's a good job the Ninja keep files on some of Ninjago's biggest villains.

SKELETONS
Alias: Skulkins
Wanted for: Attempted theft (Golden Weapons), general mayhem
Status: Unknown

LLOYD GARMADON
Alias: The Green Ninja, The Golden Ninja
Wanted for: Theft (candy), truancy, trying to resurrect a snake army
Status: Reformed

PYTHOR
Alias: Pythor P. Chumsworth
Wanted for: Theft (sealife), kidnapping, endangering the public, breaking and entering
Status: Active

NDROID
as: Mini-Nindroid
anted for: Aiding and abetting the Overlord,
nderage possession of weapons
atus: Powered down

LORD GARMADON
Alias: Sensei Garmadon
Wanted for: Endangering the public,
theft, driving an unlicensed vehicle
Status: Reformed

SKYLOR
Alias: Miss Chen
Wanted for: Espionage, theft
(elemental powers)
Status: At large, possibly reformed

MORRO
Alias: Unknown
Wanted for: Suspected evil activity,
plans unknown
Status: Serious risk to Ninjago

FIND YOUR PATH

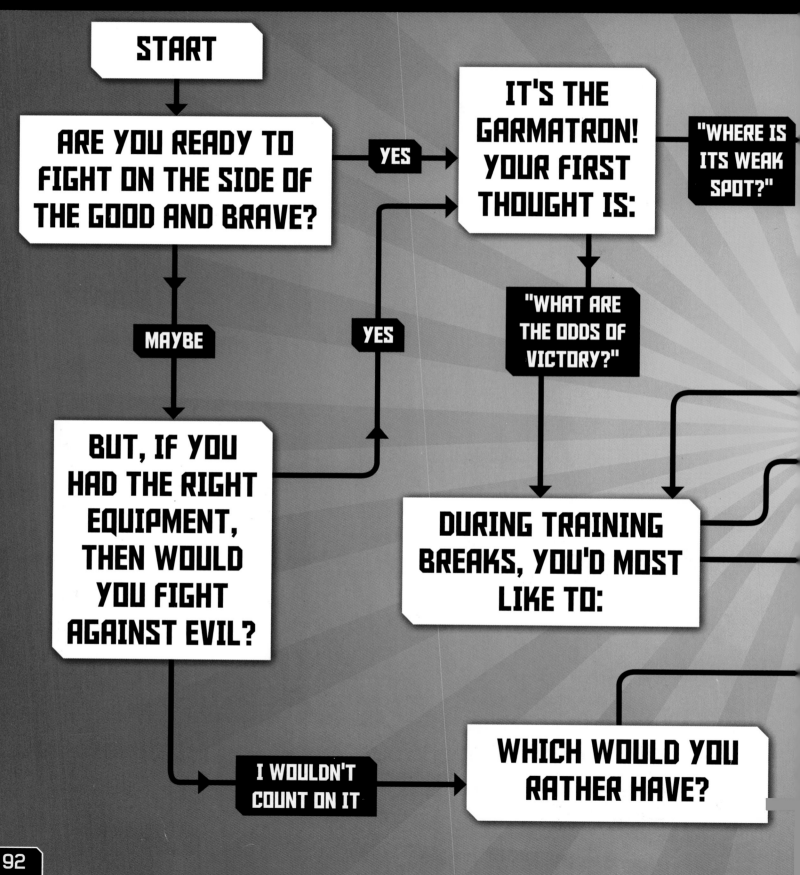

START

ARE YOU READY TO FIGHT ON THE SIDE OF THE GOOD AND BRAVE?

YES

IT'S THE GARMATRON! YOUR FIRST THOUGHT IS:

"WHERE IS ITS WEAK SPOT?"

"WHAT ARE THE ODDS OF VICTORY?"

MAYBE

YES

BUT, IF YOU HAD THE RIGHT EQUIPMENT, THEN WOULD YOU FIGHT AGAINST EVIL?

DURING TRAINING BREAKS, YOU'D MOST LIKE TO:

I WOULDN'T COUNT ON IT

WHICH WOULD YOU RATHER HAVE?

COULD YOU BE A NINJA? ANSWER THESE QUESTIONS TO FIND OUT.

YOU PREFER TO BE:

ON THE SIDELINES

SENSEI
Wise beyond your years, your intelligence and leadership help others reach their true potential.

IN THE ACTION

HANG OUT WITH FRIENDS

NINJA
A fierce fighter and a fierce friend, you'd make an awesome addition to the Ninja team.

SAMURAI
Imaginative and confident, you're perfectly suited to the solo fighting style of the Samurai.

DEVELOP A NEW INVENTION

NINDROID
Cool and calculating, with great gadgets—but will you use them for good or bad?

HIGH-TECH GADGETS

SUPERNATURAL POWERS

SNAKE
Slither on down to join the Serpentine. With your sssslippery ways, you'll fit right in!

GLOSSARY

ANACONDRAI
The most powerful of the five Serpentine tribes. Master Chen plans to revive them from near extinction.

DARK MATTER
A dangerous purple substance that has the power to turn people evil.

DIGIVERSE
A virtual universe that the Ninja enter to challenge the Digital Overlord.

DOJO
A training ground specifically designed for martial arts practice.

ELECTROCOBRAI
Snakes that live in water and carry an electrical charge. They can be used as a power source.

ELEMENTAL MASTER
An individual who wields a specific elemental power, which has been passed down through multiple generations.

FIRST SPINJITZU MASTER
A fearless warrior who created Ninjago, and banished the Overlord to the Dark Island.

FUSELAGE
The central body section of an aircraft.

GI
Loose robes worn for performing martial arts.

GOLDEN MASTER
A figure from Serpentine legend believed to bring darkness to Ninjago.

GOLDEN NINJA
The form Lloyd takes when he unlocks his true potential as the Ultimate Spinjitzu Master.

GREAT DEVOURER
The snake that bit Lord Garmadon as a child. The Serpentine later unleashed the snake on Ninjago City.

HACK
To access data in a computer or computer program, in order to make changes.

KATANA
A traditional, curved sword with a single-edged blade.

MECH
A large, mobile suit of mechanized armor.

NINDROID
A humanoid robot based on a Ninja.

NINJA
A brave warrior, trained in skills such as stealth, combat, and Spinjitzu.

NINJAGO
A world created by the First Spinjitzu Master, using the power of the Golden Weapons.

NUNCHUCKS
A weapon formed of two bars linked with a chain.

OVERLORD
The original source of darkness and evil in Ninjago. Defeated many years ago by the First Spinjitzu Master.

SAI
A dagger with two sharp blades curving outward from the hilt.

SAMURAI
A powerful warrior trained in martial arts and able to wield a variety of weapons.

SCYTHE
A tool usually used for cutting crops, but also used as a weapon. A curved blade attached to the end of a long pole.

SENSEI
A teacher or instructor of martial arts.

SERPENTINE
An ancient race of snakes, that have long inhabited Ninjago. They are divided into five distinct tribes.

SHURIKEN
A circular weapon with projecting blades, often thrown at enemies.

SKULKIN
Also known as the Skeleton Army. This evil group inhabit the Underworld.

SPINJITZU
A martial arts technique requiring the user to channel their elemental powers while spinning rapidly.

STONE ARMY
An indestructible army created using Dark Matter. Created by the Overlord to battle the First Spinjitzu Master.

TORNADO OF CREATION
A whirlwind of energy, with the power to create something new from its surroundings or own elemental power.

TRUE POTENTIAL
The highest level of power a Ninja can unlock, achieved by overcoming personal challenges.

UNDERWORLD
A realm of Ninjago inhabited by the Skeleton Army.

INDEX

Penguin
Random
House

EDITOR Pamela Afram
SENIOR DESIGNER Jo Connor
EDITORIAL ASSISTANT Beth Davies
DESIGNED BY Dynamo
COVER DESIGNED BY Sam Bartlett
PRE-PRODUCTION PRODUCER Marc Staples
SENIOR PRODUCER Lloyd Robertson
MANAGING EDITOR Simon Hugo
DESIGN MANAGER Guy Harvey
ART DIRECTOR Lisa Lanzarini
PUBLISHER Julie Ferris
PUBLISHING DIRECTOR Simon Beecroft

Additional photography by Gary Ombler

Dorling Kindersley would like to thank:
Heike Bornhausen, Randi Sørensen,
Robert Stefan Ekblom, and Paul Hansford
at the LEGO Group; Radhika Banerjee, Jon Hall,
and Pamela Shiels at DK for design assistance.

First published in the United States in 2015
by DK Publishing, 345 Hudson Street,
New York, New York 10014

15 16 17 18 19 10 9 8 7 6 5 4 3 2
004—257647—June/2015

A catalog record for this book is available from
the Library of Congress.
ISBN: 978-1-4654-2078-7

DK books are available at special discounts when
purchased in bulk for sales promotions, premiums,
fund-raising, or educational use. For details, contact:
DK Publishing Special Markets, 345 Hudson Street,
New York, New York 10014
SpecialSales@dk.com

Printed in China

A WORLD OF IDEAS:
SEE ALL THERE IS TO KNOW

www.dk.com
www.LEGO.com/ninjago